Perverted Poets

The Celebrated, Subversive, and Obscene Art of the Limerick

Limericks are art forms complex,
Their topics run chiefly to sex.
They usually have virgins,
And masculine urgings,
And other erotic effects.

Limerick, a popular form of short, funny verse that is often nonsensical and frequently vulgar, has been with us for centuries. The origin of the limerick is unknown, but it has been suggested that the name derives from the chorus of an 18th-century Irish soldiers' song, *"Will You Come Up to Limerick?"*

It is generally agreed that the limerick, though much older as a folk art, arose in English in the 18th century and it is universally agreed that they were popularized by Edward Lear in the 19th century. The first collections of limericks in English date from about 1820. Edward Lear, who composed and illustrated those in his *Book of Nonsense* (1846), claimed to have gotten the idea from a nursery rhyme beginning, "There was an old man of

Tobago." A typical example from Lear's collection is this verse:

> There was an Old Man who supposed
> That the street door was partially closed;
> But some very large rats
> Ate his coats and his hats,
> While that futile Old Gentleman dozed.

Toward the end of the 19th century and beyond, many noted men of letters -- and it's almost entirely a man's form -- indulged in the limerick.

W.H. Auden, an Oxford-education British-American poet, author, and playwright, while best known for his politically- and socially-conscious poetry and verse, also dabbled in limerick. His poetry was noted for its stylistic and technical achievement, its engagement with politics, morals, love, and religion, and its variety in tone, form and content. His limericks? Decidedly vulgar:

As the poets have mournfully sung,
Death takes the innocent young,
The rolling-in-money,
The screamingly-funny,
And those who are very well hung.

William Shakespeare's plays predate the emergence of the popular limerick, but echoes of the limerick form appear in his work, which speaks to how long limerick has existed as a folk art. In 'Othello,' Shakespeare wrote:

And let me the canakin clink, clink;
And let me the canakin clink
A soldier's a man;
A life's but a span;
Why, then, let a soldier drink.

Joseph Rudyard Kipling was an English journalist, short-story writer, poet, and novelist. He was born in India, which inspired much of his work. Kipling's works of fiction include *The Jungle Book* (1894), *Kim* (1901), and many short stories, including "The Man Who Would Be King" (1888). He, too, tried his hand at limerick:

> There was a small boy of Quebec
> Who was buried in snow to his neck.
> When they asked, "Are you friz?"
> He replied, "Yes, I is —
> But we don't call this cold in Quebec!

Charles Lutwidge Dodgson, better known by his pen name Lewis Carroll, was an English writer of children's fiction, notably *Alice's Adventures in Wonderland*. His poems *Jabberwocky* and *The Hunting of the Snark* are classified in the genre of literary nonsense. He was also a mathematician, photographer, and Anglican deacon. He was noted for his facility at word play, logic, and fantasy, so it's no surprise that he was tempted by limerick:

> There was a young lady of station
> "I love man" was her sole exclamation
> But when men cried, "You flatter"
> She replied, "Oh! no matter!
> Isle of Man is the true explanation.

Oliver Herford (1863–1935) was an American writer, artist and illustrator who has been called "The American Oscar Wilde," contributed the following limerick:

> *A damsel, seductive and handsome,*
> *Got wedged in the living room transom,*
> *When she offered much gold*
> *For release, she was told*
> *That the view was worth more than the ransom.*

Isaac Asimov was a prolific American writer and professor of biochemistry at Boston University known for his works of science fiction, like *I, Robot*, but also wrote *Lecherous Limericks*. A few of Asimov's limericks:

> *Said an ovum one night to a sperm,*
> *"You're a very attractive young germ.*
> *Come join me, my sweet,*
> *Let our nuclei meet*
> *And in nine months we'll both come to term."*

There was a sweet girl of Decatur
Who went to sea on a freighter.
She was screwed by the master
-An utter disaster-
But the crew all made up for it later.

"We refuse," said two men from
Australia,
"Bestiality this saturnalia.
For now, we bethink us,
The ornithorhynchus*
Is our down-under type of
Mammalia."

Said a certain young man with a grin,
"I think it is time to begin."
Said the girl with a sneer,
"With what? Why, your pee-er
Is scarcely as big as a pin."

* *ornithorhynchus* is the scientific name for
the platypus.

Nantucket

One of most famous American limericks begins, "There once was a man from Nantucket." In Woody Allen's 1966 film *What's Up, Tiger Lily?*, the protagonist Phil Moskowitz reads the opening line of "ancient erotic poetry": "There once was a man from Nantucket".

The animated sitcom The Simpsons makes numerous references to the limerick, such as "Thirty Minutes Over Tokyo", where Homer comments that he "once knew a man from Nantucket" but "the stories about him are greatly exaggerated".

The earliest published version of the Nantucket limerick appeared in 1902 in the Princeton Tiger written by Professor Dayton Voorhees:

> *There once was a man from Nantucket*
> *Who kept all his cash in a bucket.*
> *But his daughter, named Nan,*
> *Ran away with a man*
> *And as for the bucket, Nantucket.*

The Chicago Tribune responded with the following:

> *But he followed the pair to Pawtucket,*
> *The man and the girl with the bucket;*
> *And he said to the man,*
> *He was welcome to Nan,*
> *But as for the bucket, Pawtucket.*

Other publications seized upon the "Nantucket" motif, spawning many, many sequels:

> *Then the pair followed Pa to Manhasset,*
> *Where he still held the cash as an asset,*
> *But Nan and the man*
> *Stole the money and ran,*
> *And as for the bucket, Manhasset.*

"Of this story we hear from Nantucket,
About the mysterious loss of a bucket,
We are sorry for Nan,
As well as the man –
The cash and the bucket, Pawtucket.

But Pa's true wealth is stashed in Poughkeepsie,
Where he spends it on women and whiskey;
So Nan and her Man
Got the bucket, as planned,
But as for the fortune, Poughkeepsie

With time, Nantucket limericks became more and more vulgar, helped along by Nantucket conveniently rhyming with 'suck it' or 'fuck it':

There was a young man from Nantucket
Whose dick was so long he could suck it.
He said with a grin
As he wiped off his chin,
"If my ear was a cunt I would fuck it."

As a whole, limericks followed this path: at first, limericks were verses crowded with improbable incident and subtle innuendo, but became more and more vulgar over time, which only increased their popularity. With time, limericks have become a chiefly vulgar form of prose.

> *The limerick packs laughs anatomical*
> *Into space that is quite economical.*
> *But the good ones I've seen*
> *So seldom are clean*
> *And the clean ones so seldom are comical.*

Britain's Prime Minister, Boris Johnson, won a prize in 2016 for composing a dirty limerick about Turkish President Erdoğan having sex with a goat:

> *There was a young fellow from*
> *Ankara*
> *Who was a terrific wankerer*
> *Till he sowed his wild oats*
> *With the help of a goat*
> *But he didn't even stop to thankera.*

Johnson entered 'The Spectator President Erdoğan Offensive Poetry' competition in defense of free speech and to criticize Erdoğan's attempt to prosecute a German comedian, Jan Böhmermann, who had written an offensive joke about the Turkish President. But then, some months later, Johnson became Britain's Foreign Secretary and had to meet Erdoğan!

The political use of limerick is not confined to Britain. During the Monica Lewinsky affair, wags crafted limericks about Bill Clinton's sexual indiscretions:

"Send the missiles!" Bill cried, "On the double!
To reduce those Afghanis to rubble."
It made sense, he decided;
His missile (unguided),
Was the thing that had got him in trouble.

The president's loud protestation,
On his fall to the intern's temptation:
"This affair is still moral,
As long as it's oral.
Straight screwing I save for the nation."

As Monica held on his bum,
Bill told her to swallow his cum.
She'd later confess,
That it dripped down on her dress,
Now everyone says he was dumb.

But throughout the limerick's transformation into a ribald art form, the structure has remained the same (if flexible). The vulgarity must be delivered with wit and follow the loose rules of the form:

*The limerick's structure somewhat
necessitates **eloquent** smut.
If you haven't the time
to learn meter and rhyme,
then don't write them, you ignorant
slut.*

So what is a limerick? A limerick is a type of witty, humorous, or sometimes nonsense verse with a specific but flexible structure.

The limerick is a poem of five lines (a quintain) of anapestic or amphibrachic meter with a strict rhyme scheme of A-A-B-B-A. The three lines are trimeter (three feet, and the two B lines are dimeter (two feet).

The defining 'foot' of a limerick's meter is usually the anapaest (ta-ta-TUM), but limericks can also be considered to use the amphibrach (ta-TUM-ta).

ta-TUM-ta ta-TUM-ta ta-TUM-ta

ta-TUM-ta ta-TUM-ta ta-TUM-ta

ta-TUM-ta ta-TUM

ta-TUM-ta ta-TUM

ta-TUM-ta ta-TUM-ta ta-TUM-ta

The first line traditionally introduces a person and a place, with the place appearing at the end of the first line and establishing the rhyme scheme for the second and fifth lines. In early limericks, the last line was often essentially a repeat of the first line, although this is no longer customary.

Within the genre, ordinary speech stress is often distorted in the first line, and may be regarded as a feature of the form: "There WAS a young MAN from the coast;" "There ONCE was a GIRL from DeTROIT." Prosody is violated simultaneously with propriety.

Exploitation of geographical names, especially exotic ones, is also common, and has been seen as invoking memories of geography lessons in order to subvert the decorum taught in the schoolroom.

Historically, the exchange of limericks is almost exclusively the domain of well-educated men; the women figuring in limericks are presented almost exclusively as villains, victims, and objects of sexual desire. The most prized limericks incorporate a kind of twist, which may be revealed in the final line or lie in the way the rhymes are often intentionally tortured, or both. Many limericks show some form of internal rhyme, alliteration or assonance, or some element of word play.

The limerick as a form of doggerel poetry is essentially always transgressive in theme, and often rude. They don't have to be overtly vulgar or obscene, but the most famous ones are.

> *A limerick usually is crude.*
> *More than 50 percent are real lewd.*
> *Some don't make much sense,*
> *Even though you're not dense.*
> *...Just a whole lot of crap being spewed.*

These pages contain hundreds and hundreds of the most lewd, offensive, vulgar, and provocative limericks ever penned – and they happen to be the most clever and funny!

There was a young fellow from Slough,
who thought he was milking a cow,
until, with a shudder,
he thought 'that's no udder'.
The bull is still chasing him now.

Under the spreading chestnut tree
The village idiot sat
Amusing himself
by abusing himself
And catching it in his hat

A young woman got married in Chester.
Her mother, she kissed her and blessed her.
Says mom, "You're in luck!
He's a really good fuck!
I had him myself down in Leicester."

The girl I brought home was a prize,
With an alluring set of blue eyes,
Her breasts, so well kept,
Were what I'd expect,
But her penis was quite a surprise.

A peeker at peckers named Jay,
Hung out at the Y.M.C.A.
But the dick that he saw,
Was Detective McGraw,
Who hauled the piqued peeker away.

There once was a man from Iraq
who had holes down the length of his cock.
When he got an erection
he played a selection
from Johann Sebastian Bach.

In the Garden of Eden laid Adam
complacently stroking his madam.
and loud was his mirth,
for on all of the earth,
there were only two balls and he had them.

A dull lad from around Istanbul,
Discovered red marks on his tool,
Said the Doctor (a cynic),
"Get out of my clinic,
And wipe off that lipstick, you fool!"

There once was a young sailor from Brighton
Who remarked to his girl, "You're a tight one!"
She replied, "Bless your soul,
You're in the wrong hole.
There's plenty of room in the right one."

There once was a girl from Hoboken
Who claimed her cherry was broken
While riding her bike
on a cobblestone pike
But it really was broken from pokin'

There once was a man from Bombay
Who fashioned a cunt out of clay
The heat from his prick
Turned the clay into brick
and rubbed all his foreskin away.

There once was a clergyman's daughter
Who detested the pony he bought her,
Till she found that its dong
Was as hard and as long
As the prayers her father had taught her.

There once was a queen of Bulgaria,
Whose bush had grown hairier and hairier.
Till a prince from Peru,
Who came up for a screw,
Had to hunt for her cunt with a terrier.

There was a young dentist Malone,
who had a charming girl patient alone.
But in his depravity,
he filled the wrong cavity,
My, how his practice has grown!

There once was a whore from Peru
Who filled her vagina with glue.
She said with a grin
"If they'll pay to get in
they'll pay to get out of it too."

There once was a girl, Mary Lincoln
Whose horniness got her to drinkin'
I walked in her room
Found her riding a broom
But not in the way that you're thinkin'

There once was a whore from Sydney
Who could take it right up to her kidney
But a man from Quebec
Stuck it up to her neck
He had a big prick now didn't he?

There once was a girl from Berlin
Who was fucked by an elderly Finn
Tho' he nailed her his best
And fucked her with zest
She kept asking, "Hey Pop – is it in?"

There once was man from Calcutta
Who played with his meat in the gutter
The tropical heat
Played tricks with his meat
Instead of cream he got butter

There was a young girl of Cape Cod,
Who thought babies were fashioned by
God,
But it was not the Almighty,
Who lifted her nightie,
It was Roger the lodger, that sod!

There was a young man of Cape Horn,
Who wished he had never been born,
And he wouldn't have been,
If his father had seen,
That the end of the rubber was torn.

There was a young chap from out yonder,
Who buggered a big anaconda,
He regretted this crime,
For the rest of his time,
While the reptile grew fonder and fonder.

There was a girl, who begat,
three babies, Nat, Pat and Tat.
It was fun in breeding,
but hell in feeding.
There was no Tit for Tat.

There was a young lady named Flynn
Who said that sex is a sin
But when she was tight
It seemed quite all right
So everyone filled her with gin.

A man of the youth demographic
Would frequently stop passing traffic
When he sat with his sweet
In full view of the street
And their actions were most pornographic

A girl who was called Sara Knight,
Filled both guys and girls with delight.
Regardless of gender,
They loved to rear-end her,
And two at a time felt just right!

My mother said sex was a sin,
So I never learn how to begin.
My wife sued for divorce,
and her reason of course,
Was her only prick came from a pin.

I was thrilled when I went to the zoo:
They allowed me to bugger the gnu!
An FRZS
Informed me, "Oh yes,
It's a privilege allotted to few."

*Fellow of the Royal Zoological Society
(FRZS)

On the plains of north-central Tibet
They've come up with the weirdest thing
yet:
They pour blue enamel
Up the arse of a camel
And bugger the beast while it's wet.

There once was a girl from Madrid
Who found she was having a kid,
So she held in her water
For nine months and a quarter
And drowned the poor bastard, she did.

There once were two ladies from
Birmingham,
And this is the story concerning 'em:
They hitched up the frock
And diddled the cock
Of the Bishop, as he was confirming 'em.

There once was a fellow from Bicester
Who wanted to bugger his sister,
But, not liking dirt,
He purchased a squirt,
And rinsed out her arse with a clyster.

*A clyster is an archaic term for an enema

Said the nun, as the Bishop withdrew:
"This must be our final adieu,
For the vicar is thicker
And slicker and quicker
And six inches longer than you."

There was an old whore from Azores
Whose cunt was all covered in sores.
The dogs of the street
Wouldn't eat the green meat
That hung in festoons from her drawers.

There was a young maid of Shallott
Who lived upon shit, piss, and snot.
When these failed to please,
She'd devour the green cheese
That she scraped with a spoon from her
twat.

There was a young man from Leeds,
Who swallowed six packets of seeds.
It soon came to pass,
He was covered with grass,
And couldn't see shit for the weeds!

There was a young couple from Delhi,
That during sex used lubricating jelly,
But in their haste,
They used wallpaper paste,
And ended up stuck belly to belly.

There once was a man from Paras
And his balls were made of just pure brass
During one stormy weather
He clung them together
And lightning shot out of his ass.

There once was a man from Boston
who bought himself an Austin
He had room for his ass
and a gallon of gas
and his balls fell out and he lost 'em

Johnny come tickle me in the right place
I'll show you where
under my petticoat where there's some hair
if you don't tickle me in the right place
I'll pick up my petticoat and piss in your face

A conflicted young priest from
Southampton,
while believing all sin should be stamped on,
had been loving the strength
and the girth and the length
of the cock that his mouth had been
clamped on.

A virgin felt urged in Toulouse
Till she thought she would try self-abuse.
In search of a hard on,
She ran out to the garden,
And was had by a statue of Zeus!

A sweet young stripper named Jane
Wore five inches of thin cellophane.
When asked why she wore it,
She said, "I abhor it,
But my cunt juice would spatter like rain."

Amber (who called herself Skye),
Spread her thighs, as she said with a sigh,
"I've shaved myself bare,
to get more flow of air,
else my panties just never stay dry!"

There was a young girl named O'Hare,
Her body was covered with hair.
It was really fun,
to probe with one's gun,
'Cause her quimmy might be anywhere!

One morning while Mum was in town,
Young Duart stripped off her nightgown,
Gave step-dad a treat
Groping under his sheet,
Saying, "Since you are up, I'll go down."

There was an old lady who lay,
With her legs wide apart in the hay.
She said to the plowman,
"Come on, do it now man,
Don't wait till your hair has turned gray!"

There once was a lady from Wheeling,
Who had a funny feeling.
She laid on her back,
And tickled her crack,
And peed all over the ceiling.

Said the President to a willing young lass,
"Here's your chance to be truly first class.
It is really quite slick
To lick the first prick.
Mike and George only get to kiss ass."

There once was a woman from Rake
Who used her vagina to bake.
Like Marie-Antoinette,
She believed she'd be set
When she shouted, "Now let them eat
cake!"

There was a young man from Kildare
who was fucking a girl on a stair.
The banister broke,
but he doubled his stroke,
and he finished her off in mid-air.

There once was an anus named Jeever
Whose owner was a bible believer
He was exit only
Till his owner met Foley
And now he's become a receiver.

There one was a priest, Father Noyes,
Whose life was filled with such joys
He found his true love
In the Lord up above
And inside the pants of young boys.

The whore from next door went a'running
in a dress that was particularly stunning
the fabric that was there
was exceptionally bare
and showed off all of her cunning!

There once was a girl named Jill,
whose pussy tasted like Dill.
If I had a nickel,
For every time she had sex with a pickle,
I'd have a whole dollar bill.

Mary had a little lamb,
Its fleece was black as coal,
every time it jumped the fence,
you could see its pink asshole.

There once was a woman from Nod
whom prayed from a child from God
it wasn't the almighty
who crept up her nighty
it was the vicar the dirty old sod

There was a young lady from Lyme
who liked to have sex all the time
so she slept with a tick,
and you might say 'ick'
but she said it is divine

There once was a lady from Exeter,
so beautiful that men craned their necks at
her,
One was even so brave
as to take out and wave
the distinguishing mark of his sex at her

When she danced at the Easter Parade,
Such a sexy impression she made,
That some lads from St. Paul's,
In tight jeans, hurt their balls,
And had to be given first-aid.

This pirate (the story relates),
Just loved to go dancing on skates.
He fell on his cutlass,
Which rendered him nutless,
And virtually useless on dates.

On their first night of marital bliss,
The bride sought a genital kiss,
But OH her dismay,
When she heard hubby say,
"Ewww... not in the hole where you piss!"

There once was a beautiful lass,
Had a candle shoved right up her ass.
The flame she did see,
So she started to pee,
So she would not get burned in the pass.

There once was a dude called Trevor,
has had the same girlfriend forever,
She smells like shit,
And is missing a tit.
but gives head like a fucking endeavor.

There once was a woman named Dinah
Who had the world's smallest vagina
In fact, one coarse guy
Said it looked like the eye
Of a fellow who'd come straight from China.

There was a young fellow called Boff
Who'd smile when docs had him cough,
For as a young boy,
He ate too much soy,
And now only men get him off.

A vice both obscene and unsavory
Holds the mayor of Southampton in slavery
With bloodcurdling howls
He deflowers young owls
Which he keeps in an underground aviary

A masculine fellow named Morris
declared, when he found the clitoris,
that with this last detail,
he'd become Supreme Male,
but was kicked in the face by Chuck Norris.

My lovely young girlfriend from Boston
Said, "My salad is needing a tossin'
Stick out your tongue,
And lick out my bung,
Until then my legs will be crossin'!"

One night the old Duke of Earl
Was licking his lady's pink pearl
She said with delight
"If you do that all night,
I'll let you screw the serving girl."

There once was a man named Dave
Who kept a dead hooker in a cave
She was minus one tit
And smelled like shit
But look at the money Dave saved.

There once was a man named Bob,
whose dick was so hard it would throb.
When women wouldn't do,
all his friends knew,
that a man on his knees got the job.

There once was a hooker from Dallas,
Who used a dynamite stick as a phallus,
They found her vagina
in North Carolina,
And her asshole in Buckingham Palace.

There was a young girl from Devizes
Who had tits of different sizes
One was so small
It was nothing at all
But the other was big and won prizes

There once was a madam from Racine
Who invented a loving machine
Concave or Convex
To suit either sex
And remarkably easy to clean!

There once was a call girl named Gail
on whose chest was the price of her tail,
and on her behind,
for the sake of the blind,
was the same information in Braille.

Old Mother Hubbard went to the cupboard
To get her dog some bread
When she stooped over
Up jumped Rover
And she was bred instead

There once was a man named Dundee
Who fucked an ape in a tree.
The result was most horrid,
All ass and no forehead,
Three balls and a purple goatee!

A woman from New York named Delores
Just couldn't stop rubbing her clitoris
she said with a smile,
I've done it for quite awhile,
and if I had two vaginas it'd be glorious

A woman, her name was Mary,
I think her cunt quite scary.
For in there had been
a great number of men
And if I'd known I'd been wary.

There once was a man from Rangoon,
Who was born nine months too soon.
He hadn't the luck
to be born by a fuck.
He was scraped off the sheets with a spoon.

There once was a whore named Jess
whose fucking made quite a mess
She had some diseases
She farts when she sneezes
and I fucked her too I confess

There once was a plumber named Lee,
Who was plumbing his girl by the sea,
She said "Lee, stop your plumbing,
I hear someone coming."
"I know," said Lee, "tis me".

There's this sexy young girl named SL,
When she's horny it's easy to tell,
It isn't the sighs,
or the spreading of thighs,
Just that wonderful hot female smell.

Sweetie's a talented lass,
Her pix are just loaded with class,
She knows how to cope,
with a jerk or a dope,
She just slams a butt plug up their ass.

The most sensuous entry made Jade,
all hands stopped where they played,
But OH, our surprise,
when she snapped shut her thighs,
And explained that she'd never been laid!

Mandy's my wee Irish lass,
She's cute and her wit is a gas,
And big lips that protrude,
She could pass for a dude,
Cuz for sure she's got balls made a brass!

With her pink rubber friend named "The Pearl",
She sets the men's hormones a whirl,
They know she ain't fakin',
Cuz there's no mistakin',
The cum oozin' out of that girl!

There once was a vampire named Jud,
Whose hobby was drinking girls' blood.
'Til he clamped down on bush,
And found in the mush,
That his mouth had been filling with crud.

There once was a man named Alas
Whose balls were constructed of brass.
In stormy weather,
They clanged together
And lightning shot out of his ass.

A man who was surfing for porn
Soon found himself filled with self-scorn
For the pussy he fapped to,
Kept his attention rapt, too,
Was his mother's, from which he'd been
born

Long ago lived a woman most heinous
With her vagina reversed with her anus.
When a fellow most fair
Stuck his penis down there,
She hadn't the heart to explain it.

There once was a man name of Enis
Who with limerick writing was genius
wrote one thousand thirty
not one of them dirty
'til he noticed his name rhymed with penis

An alluring young lady from Wight
Spoonfeeds rum to her cat every night
And so, boyfriends state,
She's a good one to date,
With her pussy entrancingly tight

A Madam in Henry Ford's day
adopted that genius's way.
The first girl would suck
The second would fuck
And the third would collect all their pay.

There was a young girl from Rabat,
who had triplets, Nat, Pat and Tat;
It was fun in the breeding,
But hell in the feeding,
When she found she had no tit for Tat.

A pansy from western Khartoum,
Brought a lesbian up to his room.
They argued all night
Over who had the right
To do what, and with which, and to whom.

The was a man from Peru,
Who fell asleep in his canoe,
He dreamt that Venus,
Was tickling his penis,
And woke up with a hand full of goo.

A large peckered fella from Spain
Was so large, it caused the girls pain
It was easy to tell
That he was more well
Hung than Saddam Hussein

There once was an Indian guy
Who came from the town of Mumbai
With the size of his member
That defined his gender
He could easily poke out your eye

there once was a girl from New Zealand
who had a peculiar feelin'
she laid on her back
tickled her crack
and pissed all over the ceilin'

There once was an old man from Kent
Whose dick was so long it had bent.
He saved himself trouble
And put it in double
And instead of coming he went.

there was an old man from china
who wasn't a very good climber
he slipped on a rock
and split his cock
and now he has a vagina

There once was a woman from Montserrat,
Who lived on green apples and snot.
In the year of the freeze
she lived on the cheese
She scraped from the sides of her twat.

There once was a man named Moose
who fell in love with a goose.
They thought it alright
to screw thru the night
'til one of his nuts came loose!

There once was a girl from El Paso,
who used to do tricks with her lasso,
she would swallow the rope
and tween her legs she'd grope,
and pull it right out of her asshole!

Said the girl who was known as TX,
"My life's gotten way too complex.
There's girls, and there's boys,
And ALL of my toys.
It's TOUGH, this addiction to sex!"

Kate, as most everyone knows,
Is submissive right down to her toes,
But if you think maybe,
that you'll call her baby,
You won't get her out of her clothes.

Soft Moan likes her cyber and phone,
Though single she's never alone,
Cuz if it's for sale,
it's been up her tail,
No sex toy that she doesn't own.

Calypso's real name is Violetta,
She wants all the guys to come getta,
If you thinks she likes oral,
She'll give you a quarrel,
I guess she likes anal much betta!!

There once was a necro named Ned,
Who delighted in fucking the dead,
He went to the grave
and dug like a slave,
And that's how he came to meet Ted.

There was a young lady from Wheeling
whose body was very appealing
she laid on her back
and opened her crack
and pissed all over the ceiling

There once was a man from Korea
Who had explosive diarrhea
He had to poop
He ruined his suit
Then he died from gonorrhea

There was a young from Paris
Who wished he had a bat like Roger Maris
But when he looked down
It was not too much that he found
And then he stated that life is not the
fairest.

There once was a chef from Nottingham
Who while making eclairs would put snot in 'em.
When he ran out of snot,
Likely as not,
He'd take out his pecker and jack off a shot in em!

On the chest of a barmaid in Yale
Were tattooed the prices of ale
And on her behind
For the sake of the blind
Was the same information in braille

There was a young lass named Sally
Who enjoyed the occasional dally
She sat on the lap
Of a well-endowed chap,
and said" Ooh, you're right up my
alley!"

A man in the midst of self oral
One night tasted something quite
horrible
The cum in his nads
Had somehow gone bad
And his dick shot out something
deplorable

was a young fellow named Bliss,
Whose sex life was strangely amiss,
For even with Venus,
His recalcitrant penis,
Would seldom do better than t
h
i
s.

"Dead batteries", groaned frustrated Corrie,
As she urgently took inventory,
Of her vegetable crisper,
Then moaned in a whisper,
"I am SO hot from reading that story!"

A horny old broad named Suzanne,
Was in desperate need of a man,
Though she had one tied down,
While she took off her gown,
He got himself free and he ran.

When I was young, and in my prime
I used to masturbate all the time
Now I'm older,
I got more sense
I corn hole chickens through the
fence.

There once was a woman from
Boston
With a cunt so big, you'd get lost in
A fella so brave
He entered her cave
When he came out, he was in Austin

There once was a girl named Plum
Who drank a half quart of Rum
And a shot of whisky
Now feeling frisky
She stuck the empty bottle up her
bum!

A lady with features cherubic,
Was famed for her area pubic.
When they asked her its size,
She replied in surprise,
"Are you speaking of square feet, or
cubic?"

A woman who called herself Paige,
Exclaimed in sarcastic outrage,
"You can wonder all night
if I'm loose or I'm tight,
But you'll never use your tool as the
gauge!"

A slut named Mary, to begin,
A talented woman of sin
With a nod and a wink
She flashed some pink
And said "everyone's welcome, come
in."

A well-partied co-ed named Dawn,
When asked what conclusion she'd drawn,
Said, "I was having a ball...
But I just can't recall
this tattoo... or where all my pubic hair's gone!!"

A beat schizophrenic said, "Me?
I am not I, I'm a tree."
But another, more sane,
Shouted, "I'm a Great Dane!"
And covered his pants leg with pee.

A kinky young girl from Bordeaux,
Fell in love with a dashing young
beau.
To increase his regard,
She would squat in his yard,
And pee "I Love You" in the snow.

There was a young man from
Savannah
Who died in a curious manner:
He whittled a hole
In a telephone pole
And electrified his banana.

There once was a hermit named Dave
Who kept a dead whore in his cave.
"I know it's a sin,"
He said with a grin,
"But think of the money I save!"

While Titian was mixing rose madder,
His model reclined on a ladder.
Her position to Titian
Suggested coition,
So he leapt up the ladder and had 'er.

A pious young lady of Chichester
Made all the pale saints in their
niches stir.
And each morning at matin
Her breast in pink satin
Made the bishop of Chichester's
breeches stir.

There once was a lady of Totten
Whose tastes grew perverted and
rotten.
She cared not for steaks,
Nor for pastries, nor cakes,
But lived solely on penis au gratin.

A man called Percival Lee
Got up one night for a pee.
When he got to the loo
It was quarter to two,
And when he got back it was three.

There once was a couple named Kelly
Who walked around belly to belly
Because, in their haste,
They used library paste
Instead of petroleum jelly!

A lovely young lady named Alice
Used a dynamite stick as a phallus.
They found her vagina
In North Carolina
And bits of her titties in Dallas.

There once was a lovely young lass
Who had a magnificent ass:
Not smooth, round and pink
As you probably think,
But a rough, gray-maned cropper of grass.

There once was a man named Sweeney,
who somehow spilled gin on his weenie.
Just to be couth,
he added vermouth,
and then slipped his date a martini.

There was a young lady from Kew
Who said, as the bishop withdrew,
Oh, the Vicar is quicker,
And thicker and slicker,
And four inches longer than you.

The limerick's callous and crude,
Its morals distressingly lewd;
It's not worth the reading
By persons of breeding -
It's designed for us vulgar and rude.

There once was a man called Dave,
Who kept a dead whore in a cave,
He said "I admit,
I'm a bit of a shit,
But think of the money I save".

An architect fellow named Yoric
can, when he's feeling euphoric,
provide for selection
three types of erection:
Corinthian, Ionic, and Doric.

There once was a young girl named Jeanie
Whose Dad was terrible meanie:
He fashioned a latch,
And a hatch for her snatch -
She could only be had by Houdini!

There once was a woman from Arden
Who was seen sucking a man in the garden
Her mother said, "Flo,
Where does it all go??
And she said, "Gulp, Beg your pardon?"

There once was a fellow named Riddle,
Who's hobby was playing the fiddle.
He went into the john,
With a roaring hard-on,
And there Riddle fiddled his diddle.

There was a young man named Crockett,
Whose balls got caught in a socket.
His wife was a bitch.
And she threw the switch,
As Crockett went off like a rocket.

There was a young lady named Claire,
Who possessed a magnificent pair.
Or that's what I thought,
'Til I saw one get caught,
On a thorn, and begin to lose air!

There once was a freshman named Lin,
Whose tool was as thin as a pin,
A virgin named Joan
From a Bible belt home,
Said "This won't be much of a sin."

There was an old man of Goditch,
Had the syph and the clap and the itch.
His name was McNabs,
And he also had crabs,
The dirty old son of a bitch.

Said the Cardinal to Mother Superior,
"Your singing is just too inferior",
She, not to be crass,
Replied with some class,
"You can bloody well kiss my posterior!"

There once was a lady from Greeling,
Who claimed to have no sexual feeling.
'Till a fellow named Morris,
Explored her clitoris.
...She had to be scraped off the ceiling!!

There was a young fellow in France,
With an awfully large tool in his pants.
T'was as big as a horse,
Said the ladies, of course,
"That would kill me, but, OH, for the
chance!"

There once was a gal named Lewinsky,
Who played on a flute like Stravinsky.
'Twas "Hail to the Chief",
on this flute made of beef,
that stole the front page from Kaczynski.

There was a young priest name of Cabot,
whose libido was that of a rabbit.
He'd kiss the young nuns,
and fondle their buns,
so well that he got in the habit.

I once knew a man, made me frantic!
His member was super gigantic
He gave it a flip
(it was named for the ship)
"Would you like to go down on Titanic?"

There was a young Scotsman while dossing
Met a lass on a street he was crossing
She cried "from the angle of tilt
Of your sporran and kilt
I'd say that your caber needs tossing"

A sexy young maiden named Jill
Tried a dynamite stick for a thrill
They found her vagina
In North Carolina
And bits of her tits in Brazil

From a crypt in the church of St. Giles,
Came a scream that resounded for miles!!
"My goodness gracious!"
Said brother Ignatius.
"I forgot that your lordship has piles."

A certain young fellow from Ransome
Had a dame seven times in a hansom.
When she shouted for more,
Said he from the floor,
The name, Miss, is Simpson, not Samson.

There once was a man named Eugene
who invented a screwing machine.
Concave and convex,
it served either sex,
and played with itself in between.

There once was a Minister's daughter
who hated the pony he'd bought her,
'til she found that it's dong
was as hard and as long
as the prayers that her father had taught
her.

A pansy who lived in Khartoum,
Took a lesbian up to his room,
But, they argued all night,
Over who had the right,
To do what, and with which, and to whom.

There was a young girl of Aberystwyth
Who took grain to the mill to get grist with.
The miller's son, Jack,
Laid her flat on her back,
And united the organs they pissed with.

There was a young whore from Madrid,
Whom it was said could be bought for a
quid.
But a bastard Italian,
Who was hung like a stallion,
Said he could do her for nothing...and did!

There was a young fellow named Pfister,
Who noticed an odd sort of blister,
Where no blister should be.
What was worse - do you see? -
He had got it at home from his sister.

There once was a girl named Danielle,
Who would blush when her nipples would
swell,
But her biggest frustration,
uncontrolled flatulation,
Caused her love life to go all to hell.

There once was a fellow from Stoke
Who took a girl out for a poke
Imagine his shock
When she pulled out her cock
'Cos she wasn't a bird but a bloke

A guy with his girl in a Fiat
Said, "Where on earth is my key at?"
As he started to seek,
She let out a shriek,
"THAT'S not where it's likely to be at!"

There once was a farmer named Bill
Who used a milking machine for a thrill
He let out a great shout
When he couldn't pull it out
For it was set for a 16 quart fill

There was a young parson named Bings,
Who talked about God and such things;
But his secret desire
Was a lad in the choir,
With a bottom like jelly on springs.

There once was a fellow named Rick,
Had a girlfriend who fondled his dick.
And when it got stiff,
He entered her quiff,
And blew off his load pretty quick.

A maiden at college in Breeze,
Slept about with B.A.'s and Lit.D.'s,
But she collapsed from the strain,
Alas, it was plain,
She was killing herself by degrees.

A lady with features cherubic
Was famed for her area pubic.
When they asked her its size
She replied in surprise,
"Are you speaking of square feet, or cubic?"

There was once a lawyer named Rex,
who was small in the parts used in sex,
When charged with exposure,
He replied, with composure,
"De minimus non curat lex."

Hickory dickory dock
A slut was suckin' a cock
Her hair got tangled
The bitch got strangled
But at least she swallowed the lot

There once was a pervert from Warsaw
Who loved a ewe that he once saw
But instead of getting sleep
He'd go out and fuck sheep
And now there's a kid who goes 'paaa'.

A filthy and foul-mouthed young man
Writes limericks like all-too-few can
Heaps of cunts, shit, and cocks
For cheap prurient shocks
But the fucking things rhyme and they scan

There once was a man in Nantucket
Who took a twink to the bushes to fuck it
The boy said, "Get off me you queer,
Get away from my rear,
Come 'round to the front and I'll suck it!"

A lady while dining at Crewe
Found a horse cock 'n balls in her stew.
Said the waiter, "Don't shout,
And don't wave it about,
Or the others will all want some too."

There was a lady from Australia,
who painted her ass as a dahlia.
The shape was all right,
the colors were bright,
but the smell was a terrible failure.

There once was a fellow named Tommy,
who could deep throat a log of salami.
"It's amazing!" I spoke,
as he said with a choke,
"I first learned this trick from my mommy!"

There once was a girl from Seattle,
Whose hobby was sucking off cattle.
When a bull from the South,
Shot a load in her mouth,
Her tits started to rattle.

One morning a man named John
Discovered his penis was gone
He looked high & low
And wouldn't you know
It was sunning itself on the lawn.

The sea captain's tender young bride,
Fell into the bay at low tide.
You could tell by her squeal,
That a chance passing eel,
Had discovered a warm place to hide.

There once was a priest from Morocco
Whose motto was really quite macho
He said, "To be blunt
God decreed we eat cunt.
Why else would it look like a taco?"

There once was a lonely Canuck
Who always was down on his luck
He could not get it on
Til he slept with your mom
Now he's happy, but down twenty bucks

A bobby of Nottingham Junction,
Whose organ has long ceased to function,
Deceived his good wife
For the rest of his life
With the aid of his constable's truncheon.

There was a woman Louise,
whose cunthair hung down to her knees,
the crabs got together,
and knitted a sweater,
they called it a flying trapeze.

A rodeo clown named McDecklund
Gave sex when his wife beckoned
At the height of her flame,
He yelled her sister's name
And then tried to stay on for 8 seconds!

It seems I impregnated Marge,
So I do rather feel, by and large,
That some dough should be tendered,
For services rendered,
But I can't quite decide what to charge.

Have you heard of the unlucky abbott
with a cock that was shaped like a rabbit?
It fit in no one
'til one day a nun
with a cunt like a hutch dropped her habit.

A lady from South Carolina
placed fiddle strings 'cross her vagina.
What, with proper-sized cocks
once was sex, became Bach's
Tocatta and Fugue in D Minor.

There once was a woman from Venus
Whose body was shaped like a penis
She met a gay pair
Who said with a flair,
"I imagine she might come between us."

There once was a girl named Denise,
Who liked anal for sexual release,
But now her ass burns,
And we hope that she learns,
That anal works better with grease!!

There once was a girl from Mobile
Who was partially made out of steel.
She could only get thrills
from mechanical drills
and off-center emory wheels.

There was a young man named McTavish
who attempted an anthropoid ravish.
But his object in rape
was the wrong kind of ape
and the anthropoid ravished McTavish.

A rare old bird is the pelican,
His bill holds more than his belly can.
He can take in his beak,
Enough food for a week;
I'm damned if I know how the hell 'e can.

There once was a man from the Keys
Who said to his girl, on her knees,
"It would give me great bliss
If while playing with this
You would pay some attention to these."

I knew a vagina named Biddle
Whose hairstyle was always a riddle
She tried the hairspray
And the gel every day
But it always would part in the middle

There was a man from Brazil
Who swallowed a dynamite pill
his stomach perspired,
his ass backfired
And his dick shot over the hill

Said an ovum one night to a sperm,
You're a very attractive young germ!
Come join me my sweet,
Let our nuclei meet,
And in nine months we shall both come to
term.

There was a young women of Cheadle,
Who once gave the clap to a beadle.
Said she, "Does it itch?"
"It does, you damned bitch,
And it burns like hell-fire when I peedle."

Said Bill Clinton to young Ms. Lewinsky,
"We don't want to leave clues like
Kaczynski,
Since you look such a mess,
use the hem of your dress,
And wipe that stuff off of your chinsky!!"

A gay Irish Priest in New Delhi
Tattooed the Lord's Prayer on his belly
The time that a brahman
Got down to the Amen
He'd blown both salvation and Kelly.

There once was a monk in Siberia
with morality rather inferior.
He did to a nun
what he shouldn't have done,
and made her a Mother Superior.

There was a young lady from Kent
Who found that she couldn't pay rent
To her landlord she owed
So upon him she rode
'Till she AND her money were spent

There once was a pervert named Manny,
Who stuck his long dick up his fann,y
Oh, what's this shouting about?
Seems he can't get it out.
He can't shit, he can't piss, it's uncanny!

There was an old lady from wheeling,
she had such a wonderful feeling.
She lay on her back,
spread open her crack
and came all over the ceiling.

A popular girl named Lucille,
Performed oral with uncommon zeal,
But she seldom swallowed,
Cuz the one rule she followed,
Was to brush after every meal.

There was young lady from Ongar,
Who made love in the sea with a conger.
They asked, "How does it feel
To make love with an eel?"
She said, "Like a man only longer!"

There once was a pirate named Lunt,
While fucking, he said with a grunt:
"With a wiener that's wooden,
I can't feel your puddin,"
Said she, "You've splintered me cunt."

A mathematician named Hall
possessed an octagonal ball.
The square of its weight
plus his penis plus eight
is his phone number give him a call.

My back aches, my penis is sore;
I simply can't fuck any more;
I'm dripping with sweat
and you haven't come yet
And good God, it's a quarter to four!

A wanton young lady from Wimley
Reproached for not acting quite primly
Said, "Heavens above!
I know sex ain't love,
But it's such an entrancing facsimile."

There was an old Count of Swoboda,
Who would not pay a whore what he owed
her.
So with great savoir-faire,
She stood on a chair,
And pissed in his whiskey-and-soda.

There was a young fellow named Baker,
Who seduced a vivacious young Quaker.
And when he had done it,
She straightened her bonnet,
And said: "I give thanks to my Maker."

A president we shall call "Billy",
Whose escapades, we think quite silly,
Was finally sued,
For his antics were crude,
But the young girl was thrilled with his willy.

There once was a man named McNamater,
With a tool of prodigious diameter.
It wasn't the size
that gave girls surprise,
But his rhythm... iambic pentameter.

There was a cute girl named Raspberry,
whom I met while she still had her cherry,
I haven't a clue,
why my fingers turned blue,
But damn, it was real fuckin' scary!

There was a young fellow named Lancelot
Whom his neighbors all looked on askance a
lot.
Whenever he'd pass
A presentable lass,
The front of his pants would advance a lot.

There was a young lady named Hitchin,
Who was scratching her crotch in the
kitchen.
Her mother said, "Rose,
It's the crabs, I suppose."
She said, "Yes, and the buggers are itchin'!!"

A luscious psychotic named Jane,
Once sucked every man on a train.
Said she, "Please don't panic,
I'm just nymphomanic,
This wouldn't be fun were I sane."

There was a young girl from Madrass,
That had a magnificent ass.
You probably think,
it was soft and pink,
But was gray, had ears, and ate grass.

There once was a rabbi named Keith,
Who circumcised men with his teeth.
It was not for the leisure,
Or the sexual pleasure,
But to get at the cheese underneath.

There once was a priest from Morocco,
Whose motto was really quite macho.
He said, to be blunt,
"God decreed we eat cunt!
Why else would it look like a taco?

There once was a woman named Jill,
Tried a dynamite stick for the thrill,
They found her vagina,
In South Carolina,
And bits of her tits in Brazil!

Said a woman with open delight,
My pubic hair's perfectly white.
I admit there's a glare,
But the fellows don't care
They locate it more quickly at night.

There was a young girl in Reno,
Who lost all her dough playing keno.
But she lay on her back,
Exposing her crack,
And now she owns the casino.

There once was a Senator from Mass,
Who wanted a strange piece of ass.
He lucked up and found it,
But fucked up and drowned it,
And now his future is past.

There was a young girl named Ann Heuser,
Who swore that no man could surprise her.
But Pabst took a chance,
Found a Schlitz in her pants,
And now she is sadder Budweiser.

A foolish young lady named Alice,
Used a dynamite stick as a phallus.
They found her vagina,
In North Carolina,
And her asshole in Buckingham Palace.

Lewinsky and Clinton have shown,
What Kaczynski must surely have known:
That an intern is better,
Than a bomb in a letter,
Given the choice of how to be blown.

The sea captain's tender young bride
fell into the bay at low tide,
You could tell by her squeals,
that some of the eels
had discovered a good place to hide.

There once was a gaucho named Bruno,
Who said, "about fucking, I do know...
That women are fine,
And sheep are divine,
But llamas are numero uno!!!"

If intercourse gives you thrombosis,
While abstinence causes neurosis,
I'd prefer to expire,
Fulfilling desire,
Than live on in a state of psychosis.

There was a young lady in France,
Who hopped on a bus in a trance.
Three passengers fucked her,
Besides the conductor,
And the driver shot twice in his pants.

There once was a vampire named Mable,
whose periods were really quite stable.
And every full moon,
she'd get out a spoon
and drink herself under the table.

She married a fellow named Tony
Who soon found her fucking the pony.
Said he, "What's it got,
My dear, that I've not?"
Sighed she, "Just a yard-long bologna."

There was a young lady of Natchez
Who chanced to be born with two snatches,
And she often said, "Shit!
Why, I'd give either tit,
For a man with equipment that matches."

There once was a girl named Hortense.
The size of her breasts was immense.
One day playing soccer,
Out popped her left knocker,
And she kicked it right over the fence.

Two lesbians north of the town,
Made sixty-nine love on the ground.
Their unbridled lust
Leaked out in the dust
And made so much mud that they drowned!

The ancient and tragic King Lear
Went out on the heath full of fear.
Instead of his howling,
And whining and yowling,
He should have gone out for a beer.

An insomniac young fellow named Hatches
Took a room in a whorehouse in Natchez
He still tossed and turned
half the night, but he learned
How to manage by sleeping in snatches.

There was a young maid from St. Jude,
Who attended a show in the nude.
A man in the front
said, "I think I smell cunt!"
Just like that, right out loud -- fucking rude!!

Creating Your Own Limerick

As you can see, limericks are one of the popular poetic forms because they are short, rhyming, funny, and have a bouncy rhythm that makes them easy to memorize. They're also wonderfully ribald!

Now it's your turn to write your own limericks.

The Rules of Limericks

Limericks, like all poetic forms, have a set of rules that you need to follow. The rules for a limerick are fairly simple:

- They are five lines long.
- Lines 1, 2, and 5 rhyme with one another.
- Lines 3 and 4 rhyme with each other.
- They have a distinctive rhythm (which I'll explain shortly)
- They're funny!

Of course, limerick rules are meant to be broken (or at least bent a little) if it's necessary.

Rhyming a Limerick

The rhyme scheme of a limerick, as describing in the first chapter, is known as "AABBA." This is because the last words in lines 1, 2, and 5 rhyme. Those are the "A's" in the rhyme scheme. The "B's" are the last words of lines 3 and 4. Let me give you an example:

> *There once was a man from O'Keefe*
> *Who sat on his set of false teeth*
> *He said, with a start,*
> *"Oh Lord, Bless my Heart,*
> *I've bitten myself underneath!"*

Notice that the words, "O'Keefe," "teeth," and "underneath" all rhyme. Those are the "A" words in the "AABBA" rhyme scheme. Also notice that "start" and "heart" rhyme. Those are the "B" words in the rhyme scheme.

Limerick Rhythm

Now let's take a look at the rhythm of the limerick, which is called "anapaestic.".

When you read or recite a limerick, the first two lines and the last line have three "beats" in them, while the third and fourth lines have two "beats." In other words, the rhythm of a limerick looks like this:

da DUM da da DUM da da DUM

da DUM da da DUM da da DUM

da DUM da da DUM

da DUM da da DUM

da DUM da da DUM da da DUM

The rhythm doesn't have to exactly match this, but it needs to be close enough that it sounds similar when you read it. For example, using the limerick above about the fellow from Hall, if we emphasize the beats, it reads like this:

There ONCE was a MAN from O'KEEFE

Who SAT on his SET of false TEETH

He SAID, with a START

OH LORD, bless my HEART

I've BITTEN myself underNEATH

Let's take a look at another famous limerick:

> There was an old man of Nantucket
> Who kept all his cash in a bucket;
> But his daughter, named Nan,
> Ran away with a man,
> And as for the bucket, Nantucket.

If you emphasize the beats when you read it, it comes out like this:

there WAS an old MAN of NanTUCKet

who KEPT all his CASH in a BUCKet;

but his DAUGHTer, named NAN,

ran aWAY with a MAN,

and AS for the BUCKet, NanTUCKet.

Limerick Convention

More often than not, the first line of a limerick ends with a person's first name or the name of a place. And the last line is usually funny.

Because the first line is usually the name of a person or place, writing the first line is the easiest part. You simply pick the name of a place or person – like "York" or "Joe" – and write a line like this:

There once was a lady from York

Or:

There was an old man named Joe

Then go to your rhyming dictionary and start looking for rhymes like "cork," "fork," "pork," "stork," or "snow," "blow," "flow," and so on to find more words to complete your limerick. Keep in mind that many limericks alter or exaggerate the pronunciation of words to make them rhyme.

For example, in this limerick, 'Calcutta' rhymes with 'butter':

There once was man from Calcutta
Who played with his meat in the gutter
The tropical heat
Played tricks with his meat

Instead of cream he got butter

Once you've found some rhyming words, you'll want to start thinking about a funny ending for your poem. While it may seem obvious to start with the punchline, its actually often easier to write the opening lines (1, 2, and 5), and then to fill in lines 3 and 4 afterward.

Your Turn

Now it's your turn to see if you can write a limerick of your own.

Remember to follow these steps:

- Choose the name of a person or place for the first line.
- Enter your person or place name in an online rhyming dictionary to find words that match.
- Write line 2 and 5 to rhyme with the first line.
- Now write lines 3 and 4 with a different rhyme.

When you are done writing, read your limerick out loud to see if it has the right rhythm; three "beats" on lines 1, 2, and 5, and two "beats" on lines 3 and 4, as shown above. If not, see if you can rewrite some words to get the rhythm right.

Limericks Take Practice

Writing great limericks is actually very tricky, which is why accomplished poets have enjoyed the form so much. It's not as easy as it looks! Getting the structure, rhyming, and, most of all, vulgar humor quite right takes lots of practice. But soon you'll have your audience roaring with laughter. Enjoy!

 **MAD COMEDY** hopes you enjoyed this collection of limericks and learned something of the process to create your own. As always, a five-star review on Amazon is appreciated!

Made in the USA
Las Vegas, NV
24 September 2024

95718798R00163